The Proper Care of
BICHONS FRISES

TW-136

Facing Page: Three future Diamant Champions at 8 weeks old. Photo by Missy Yuhl.

© 1996 by T.F.H. Publications, Inc.

Distributed in the UNITED STATES to the Pet Trade by T.F.H. Publications, Inc., One T.F.H. Plaza, Neptune City, NJ 07753; distributed in the UNITED STATES to the Bookstore and Library Trade by National Book Network, Inc. 4720 Boston Way, Lanham MD 20706; in CANADA to the Pet Trade by H & L Pet Supplies Inc., 27 Kingston Crescent, Kitchener, Ontario N2B 2T6; Rolf C. Hagen Inc., 3225 Sartelon St. Laurent-Montreal Quebec H4R 1E8; in CANADA to the Book Trade by Vanwell Publishing Ltd., 1 Northrup Crescent, St. Catharines, Ontario L2M 6P5 ; in ENG-LAND by T.F.H. Publications, PO Box 15, Waterlooville PO7 6BQ; in AUSTRALIA AND THE SOUTH PACIFIC by T.F.H. (Australia), Pty. Ltd., Box 149, Brookvale 2100 N.S.W., Australia; in NEW ZEALAND by Brooklands Aquarium Ltd. 5 McGiven Drive, New Plymouth, RD1 New Zealand; in Japan by T.F.H. Publications, Japan—Jiro Tsuda, 10-12-3 Ohjidai, Sakura, Chiba 285, Japan; in SOUTH AFRICA by Lopis (Pty) Ltd., P.O. Box 39127, Booysens, 2016, Johannesburg, South Africa. Published by T.F.H. Publications, Inc.

MANUFACTURED IN THE
UNITED STATES OF AMERICA
BY T.F.H. PUBLICATIONS, INC.

The Proper Care of
BICHONS FRISES

By Ann Hearn

A very studious Bichon pores over a Hemingway novel.

Contents

Ch. Chaminade Little Fugue. Owned by Michael and Terry Ravin. Photo by Missy Yuhl.

Introduction

A small, sturdy, white powderpuff of a dog, with a merry temperament evidenced by a jaunty plumed tail...one should settle for nothing less. These are words from the official American Kennel Club standard of the Bichon Frise. This playful and affectionate dog is one

Ch. Dibett Rachimaninoff Concerto and Ch. Dibett Attention Please as puppies.

of the most delightful companions one could choose to live with. The Bichon Frise is intelligent, without being aggressive; eager to please, without being wimpy; a loving companion, without being cloying; and beautiful, with the added bonus of being a pleasure to behold.

The Bichon Frise is one of the most delightful little companions one could choose to live with.

Bichons are affectionate, playful, eager to please, and a pleasure to behold.

ARE YOU A RESPONSIBLE PET OWNER?

When buying a puppy, who is a living, loving, and dependent being, a family decision should be made as to who will be the puppy's main provider. This position usually is designated to the person who is at home the most. It is true that a dog will

This Bichon fits right in with the family.

only mean feeding, providing fresh water, and bathing, but also training, loving, and sharing all responsibilities as well. It is not an ideal situation if the father and children want a dog, but the mother, who is at home the most, doesn't want the added responsibility of a pet.

If this is the case, a conflict situation would arise within the family structure, and without a doubt, the dog would be the loser. Unless all family members buy into the real "ownership" of a dog, which includes the dog's physical comforts as well as his and your emotional reward, then perhaps a pet is not for your family.

If you are a single

The Bichon is both affectionate with and protective of their young family members.

person looking for a companion, there is nothing better than coming home to the happy wagging of a tail and almost-smiling face of a Bichon. This means that you are the only one who shoulders the responsibility of dog ownership. If you are a successful career person who travels, entertains in the evenings, or works late at the office, you must realize that the life of your little companion is dependent on you for exercise, food, fresh water, medical attention when needed, proper

Dove Cote's Ziggy with owner Patty Riccio.

Dove Cote's White Tornado with owner Lynne Haberstock at their first match show.

training, and love. This means that instead of going out to dinner with friends straight from work, you must schedule a run by your home to see to the needs of your pet. The emotional reward of owning a pet must be realized along with the dedication and responsibility that comes with pet ownership.

Ch. Dove Cote Traveling Man with Malessa Hyde.

IS A BICHON FRISE THE DOG FOR YOU?

The Bichon Frise is the perfect little pet. He does not demand a large area for exercise, is not costly to feed, is eager to please, is flexible, likes all humans and other dogs, and enjoys the careful playfulness of children. He may look soft and fragile, but under that gorgeous white coat is a body that has sturdy bone structure and is steady on his feet.

The Bichon is not a sickly or disease-prone dog.

When considering a Bichon, you should also take into account the required routine care of the coat. Which member of the family is going to learn the proper brushing techniques and has the time to provide this maintenance on a weekly basis? It is this personal touch that creates a friendship between owner and dog, which offers a special reward in exchange for the time put into this effort.

The Bichon enjoys the careful playfulness of children. Dove Cote's Barley White.

In many breeds there is a definite difference in temperament, personality traits, and compatibility between males and females. Another plus for the Bichon Frise is that there is no difference in the attitudes of the sexes. A male is just as easy to live with as a female.

If you have a female, you will, upon

Male or female, the Bichon is a pet with a merry temperament and is very easy to live with. Owner, Susan Solen.

Two Bichons are better than one! These two Dove Cote puppies are owned by Karen Pecker.

her maturity (about 12 to 15 months of age), start dealing with her "seasons" or estrous cycle. This occurs about every six months and is a signal to all male dogs nearby that she is ready to be bred. The cycle lasts approximately three weeks each season— one week coming in, one week showing color, and one week going out. A female may conceive puppies at any time during this time period.

Am/Can. Ch. Norvic's Easy Does It, ROM.

Nothing is more frustrating, more work, or more expensive than an unwanted pregnancy.

If you still feel that you want a female, you should schedule to have her spayed when she reaches about two years of age. You will still go through two to three seasons, and at this time everyone in the family must be extremely careful not to let her out or let a male dog of any breed near her. When it is time for a female to be bred, the male dog will forego eating, sleeping, and being a companion until he has accomplished what he was put on this earth to do. This is instinctive and cannot be changed.

A male dog sometimes feels the need to "mark his territory" by lifting his leg on the corners of the sofa or his favorite

The Bichon Frise is an easy-to-please pet that finds comfort in any home.

This Bichon is all pupped out after a birthday bash. Owner, SanDon Bichons.

person's chair in order to let any other animals in the house know that this space is his. This usually never starts if the male dog is a young puppy when brought into his new surroundings. If the male dog is used for breeding purposes after maturity, he may feel the need to

An elegant Bichon Frise with her owner, Mary Vogel.

Two Bichon bleacher bums on their way to a Cubs game. DeAnna's De La Creme and Creme's Bella Force DeAnna. Photo by Jim Flynn.

mark. It is not advisable to have visiting male dogs brought into the living area of your home for this reason. Neutering a male dog may stop the marking of his area and may make him disinterested in wandering, if he is prone to that, but not always.

Chaminade Improvisation and Ch. Chaminade Little Fugue sit together peacefully. Owner, Barbara Stubbs. Photo by Missy Yuhl.

Ch. Deja Vu Delphinum, mother of five Champions.

The Bichon Search

Buying a puppy should not be an impulsive endeavor; it is never wise to rush out and buy just any puppy that catches your shopping eye. The more time and thought you invest, the greater your satisfaction with your new companion. And if this new companion is to be purely a pet, its background and early care will affect its future health and good temperament. It is always essential that you choose a properly raised puppy from healthy, well-bred stock. You must seek out an active, sturdy puppy with bright eyes and an intelligent expression.

Though basically a house dog, the Bichon does enjoy time outdoors.

If the puppy is friendly, that's a major plus, but you don't want one that is hyperactive nor do you want one that is dull and listless. The premises should be clean, by sight and smell, and the proprietors should be helpful and knowledgeable and want customers satisfied and will therefore represent the puppy fairly. Let good common sense guide your purchase, and choose a reliable,

Buying a puppy should not be an impulsive endeavor. Patiently sift through several litters until you find just the right one.

Avoid the hyperactive pup and the listless one; try to find one in between. Ch. Deja Vu Che Sara Sara and Ch. Deja Vu Louis of Desert Snow.

well recommended source that you know has well-satisfied customers. Don't look for a bargain, since you may end up paying many times over in future veterinary bills, not to mention disappointment and heartache if your pet does not turn out well.

There are several ways you can start your search for just the right Bichon. If your town or a larger

When searching for a puppy, don't look for a bargain. The money you save now will be spent later in veterinary costs. Two Doris Hyde pups at 6 weeks.

city nearby has an all-breed kennel club, you should contact them for the name, address, and phone number of members who breed Bichons. If you don't have the name of a kennel club, you can contact The American Kennel Club, 51 Madison Avenue, New York, New York 10010 (212 696-8200) and ask them for all-breed

Contacting a kennel club is a good place to start when you begin your Bichon search.

Ch. Sandcastle Gold Coast Jam'bre, owned by Linda Dickens.

and will not be found in all areas. Responsible breeders keep a tight rein on where their puppies go, especially females, to protect the breed from over-population. If you are more flexible in which sex puppy you want, you will have an easier search.

Start writing and calling each breeder name you receive. Be up front and tell the breeder exactly what you are looking for. If you have been to some dog shows and think you might be interested in showing your dog, you first

Responsible breeders keep a tight rein on where their puppies go, especially females, to protect from over-population.

need to learn the ways of the dog show sport, develop an eye for breed type, learn detailed grooming techniques, and learn handling skills. Buying your first Bichon may not be the best time to consider a show dog.

Over the phone the breeder is going to want to know certain things about you and your family:

1. Do you have a fenced-in yard? Many breeders will not sell to a home without a yard that protects their puppy. If you

Many breeders will not sell to a home without a fenced-in yard. Be sure you have a safe outdoor environment before you get a Bichon.

A trustworthy breeder will be interested in where his puppies are going, and may have more questions for you than you have for him.

live in an apartment, are you prepared to walk your pet regularly each day, even in bad weather?

2. Are there little children in the family? Who will teach the children proper handling and caring of the puppy? Even though the Bichon is

Your breeder will want to know if there are children in the home, and that they will be taught proper handling and caring of the pup.

a sturdy, hardy breed, they can "break" with overly-rough treatment. No tail pulling, coat grabbing, sticking fingers in the eyes, nose, nor mouth, and no teasing.

3. If you want a female, when will you have her spayed? Many breeders have a contract that requires spaying/neutering of their pet Bichons. This is a binding, legal document that *can* be

enforced. Again, the purpose of these stringent measures is to protect the breed from over-population and improper future breedings.

A breeder wants to know that you intend to be a responsible owner, that you understand and acknowledge that the puppy is a life you are willing to take into your home, and that you are committed to his care, training, and pleasure until his natural death—from the puppy housetraining through the comfortable mature years, to the aged, senile special-care years. Buying a puppy is not an impulse purchase but an agreement to share your life with your pet for as long as possible. A responsible breeder also wants to be the first one that you contact should something occur that prevents you from keeping your Bichon.

Ch. Sandcastle Island Jewel, owned by Linda and Nancy Dickens.

Surprise from Santa!

The Bichon Frise Club of America, Inc. (BFCA) provides a Rescue Service for unwanted Bichons. Rather than have dogs who are mistreated, abused, neglected,

Ch. Fran-Dors Esprit Enjoue, bred by Doris Homsher and owned by Anne Jones.

and devastated, they will take them—even sick ones—treat them, neuter them, groom them, and find excellent, caring permanent homes for them. For the most part, these Bichons are older but can make wonderful pets, as the Bichon easily changes alliance and adapts to a new home and new surroundings. Contact the BFCA for Bichon Rescue Service.

If you leave a message on a breeder's answering machine stating that

Sometimes this particular Bichon can be a real witch. Owner, Ann Freeman.

Ch. Sandcastle Bikini and Ch. Sandcastle Gold Coast Dixie.

you are searching for a Bichon as a pet, they may not return your call, especially if it's long distance, because they don't have what you want at that time. Don't be disturbed by the seeming lack of courteousness, as they probably get two to three phone calls per day like yours and are just unable to contact each caller. However, if you've heard only positive

All this Bichon Frise needs now is a set of bagpipes.

breeders in the country and you are willing to put your name on their waiting list, then by all means, persevere and call again in a few days. Sometimes this is the smartest way to go and it is well worth the wait.

It cannot be stressed enough here that buying from a *responsible* breeder is the way to obtain a purebred dog, especially one you may intend to show or breed. A breeder not only knows his bloodlines and knows the good things as well as not-so-good things about his line, but he can also evaluate a puppy at a young age and give

and glowing comments about this one breeder, or find that you are fortunate enough to live near one of the top you a pretty good idea of what the puppy will be like upon maturity. A breeder who is constantly attempting to improve his bloodline by breeding to good quality dogs (which can involve shipping his female across the country for breeding), showing his dogs at American Kennel Club-sanctioned dog shows, and obtaining championships on dogs who he has bred is the definition of a responsible breeder. He also takes great care of his puppies' health and socialization. He is

A good breeder knows his bloodlines and can give a reliable evaluation of a young puppy.

careful about who he sells his puppies to and avoids leaving them in the hands of someone who merely breeds any male to any female just to sell the puppies. He actively participates in the protection of not only his dogs but other breeds as well. He involves himself in his national breed club, his local all-breed club, and any other organization that will help continue his

A fenced-in yard is a necessity when owning a Bichon puppy.

Ch. Parfait Vision of Love. Owner, Joanne Spilman.

education in breeding and exhibiting better dogs. It takes a great deal of time, patience, money, and commitment to become a responsible breeder. They are not on every

Doris Hyde with a few of her Bichons. Breeding is an expensive endeavor, and breeders rarely make a profit on their dogs.

street corner and you should be weary of the person that claims all of his puppies can be shown to championship status, as that is untrue.

Many people think that there is great money to be made in the breeding of purebred dogs. Nothing could be further from the truth. The equipment alone is costly, traveling to dog shows every weekend all over the country is very expensive, and proper maintenance of healthy dogs is not cheap. Once you have won at a dog show, it is only natural that you want the dog world to know about it and advertising in the many dog-related publications is as costly as you might expect. There is also the added expense of maintaining puppies who don't sell due to an economy slump or a glut in your area of puppies. The health needs of an individual puppy requiring special care is also costly. Making a profit is a rare occurrence for a good, responsible dog breeder.

Buying from a breeder gives you a resource for future

When paying a high price for a pup, remember what you are buying: the good genetic history of a purebred.

Ch. Gaylors Mr. Magic of Glenelfred. Owner, Gail Antetomaso.

Ch. Sandcastle Gold Coast Dixie, owned by Linda Dickens and Deedy Pierce.

questions, leadership, help, and problem solving. Utilizing the many years of experience of a responsible breeder is worth every dollar paid for the puppy because that is actually what you are buying—the good genetic history of the dog, the knowledge of how to continue his good status, and a place to turn to for help if you need it.

What keeps a breeder involved in the sport is the love of creating something better than before, the competitive spirit, the friendships made all

Creme De La Creme II wakes up from a nap. Owner, Carol Haines.

over the world, the love of travel, the release from the pressures of the everyday job, and the need to have some control and commitment in one's life. In the dog show hobbyist's gypsy or nomadic way of life, the dog exhibiting/breeding sport offers a stability and family atmosphere not found in many other involvements.

Ch. Seastar's In A Heartbeat. Owner, L. Matlock.

Three Bichon puppies wreaking havoc on a rocking horse.

Choosing a Bichon Puppy

All recognized purebred dogs have a written description of what each breed must look like and the breed's characteristics, called a breed standard. Before you begin to visit kennels and look at Bichons, you should have a copy of the standard. Read it and try to visualize what is required. All breeders must closely follow the

A pair of three week old puppies snuggle together.

specifications set forth in this verbiage. It is from this breed standard that judges select the winners. It is the final word and criteria and only the national breed club can change it, and then only after lengthy discussion and a full membership vote. It is not easily or frequently changed. Because the Bichon is new to the American scene we have gone through two changes and one additional change required by AKC to comply with

Review the Bichon Frise standard before picking your pup. Am/Can. Ch. Norvic's Easy Does It, owned by Linda Kendall.

Ch. Sandcastle Gold Coast Dixie, owned by Linda Dickens and Deedy Pierce.

their format. This is not unusual for a new breed. Americans always seem to take their start from the Europeans and embellish it to the maximum.

You should also read books about Bichons and look at pictures of good Bichons. The corresponding secretary of The Bichon Frise Club of

Ch. Dove Cote's Mr. Magoo, owned and bred by Doris and Meg Hyde.

America, Inc. can provide you with a current reading list and a list of all local/ regional Bichon breed clubs. Try to go to a dog show or two to see a well-presented specimen. Once you have all of this information in your mind's eye, you will be able to make an intelligent choice.

Purchasing a puppy is a very emotional buy and it is hard to walk away from that sweet little face with the big dark eyes that just beg for you to take him home. Do not let the breeder frighten you into believing that this is the best puppy for the price, the only puppy available in the area, and that they have ten other buyers just waiting for you to decide. Believe me when I tell you there are other Bichons to choose from and all you have to do is locate them. That may not be as easy as going to your nearest shopping mall, but it is certainly the smartest way to shop. Please remember that you are not buying a quick, disposable, herc-today and gone-

Purchasing a pup is an emotional experience. Try not to let puppy dog eyes get the best of your dollars and sense.

Take me home, please!

tomorrow commodity; you are committing to the parenthood of a dependent life.

Make an appointment to visit the puppies. Request up front that you would like to see the entire litter at one time. Watch the puppies play a while. Which one is the most assertive? the most daring? the most confident? This is not always a true test, as the most aggressive puppy in the litter may merely be sleepy and not at his outgoing best, but it's a good way to observe. You may want to come back in a week and watch them again. The best age to evaluate Bichons is exactly on their eight-week birthday. At this age, they are generally miniatures of what they will be at maturity.

Some of the puppies may be all white, some a creamier cast, and some may even have spots of biscuit, beige, or even red/orange. These spots are usually around the head and upper body. Do not be concerned in the least, as almost all Bichons fade to all

Although these Bichon puppies may appear identical, each one has his own individual personality.

white at maturity. It is usually the breeder's opinion that the puppy with color in its coat will end up having the best pigment around the eyes, nose, and feet. The whiter coats are usually the straighter, longer,

If possible, try to see an entire litter and pick the pup that stands out to you.

more open coats and take much longer to develop. Both are absolutely correct, providing the coats do not part at the neck and look sparse enough to cause concern that the mature coat will also be fine and open. It is the adult undercoat that forces the outer, longer coat to stand out in the powder-puff look.

If you do not know how to look at a puppy bite to see if the teeth meet in the proper scissor placement, ask the breeder to show you the bite. If you are considering a male, ask if he is "complete," which means that he has both testicles in the proper position.

Ch. Miri-Cals Shenanigans catches 20 winks. Owner, Miriam C. Barnhart.

Check the tummy for a hernia caused by

Ch. Bella Angelina of Deja Vu ROM. Owner, L. Matlock.

beginning just above the eyes. Standing on the side of the puppy you should be able to see a good length of neck and a shortish back, with legs as long as the depth of the body. It is this equal look of legs to body depth and neck to length of back that gives the Bichon his essence. The tail-set and carriage should be up, over, and hung down the left side of the body, with the rear legs able to stand just beyond the "buns" of the dog. The front legs should be straight and on a puppy will be slightly closer together than they will be when the chest has developed. Most importantly, does the

eye to appear forward looking and not curved around the side of the head. The muzzle is shorter than the skull by two-thirds and the skull is slightly rounded, with the ears

puppy look balanced, happy, healthy, and eager?

Puppies should not leave their first home environment before the age of ten weeks and preferably twelve weeks if you have never had the responsibility of a puppy before. This is not a universally agreed-upon statement, as the researchers state that a puppy attaches to his new owners best at six to seven weeks, but they also state that a puppy, when taken from his mother and litter mates too early, will become a neurotic adult. A Bichon puppy is not totally weaned from his mother until he is approximately

An example of a happy, healthy, and balanced Bichon puppy. Owner, Jean Glass.

five weeks of age. He hasn't had a full complement of protective immunizations until twelve weeks and his security, seated in the warmness of litter mates and mother, has not been fully established until ten weeks.

After you have watched the entire litter, ask the breeder to take away the ones not available to you, certain show puppies, the ones the breeder is keeping, and the opposite of whichever sex you have selected. Now you will see the puppies who are available to you.

When it is time for you to make your decision, pick the puppy who pleases your eye, whose personality complements your lifestyle, and whose price is best for your pocketbook.

Puppies who are taken from their first home environment before the age of 10 weeks could become neurotic as adults. Owner, R. Kendall.

Facing Page: *Snowberry's Sabra Bronson at 7 months. Owner, Robert Kendall.*

Ch. Tomaura Shevaun of Snowberry.

Bringing Your Bichon Home

Prior to the exciting day when your new puppy comes home to live with you, you should have everything ready for his arrival. Talk to the breeder to find out what his diet has been so that you may have his food ready. It is not wise to make a sudden change in diet, as this can cause diarrhea and make his first days very unpleasant for both you and him. Go to

Bichon puppy sleeps next to his new friend.

the pet supply store and purchase a feeding dish and a water dish as large as an adult Bichon will require—approximately a two-cup capacity. It is advisable to get stainless steel dishes, as some breeders feel the plastic tends to lighten the nose and, after the plastic becomes rough with wear and tear, breaks off the facial coat of the Bichon. Also the puppy may think a plastic dish is a great chewing toy, but actually it is not safe at all.

Stainless steel water and food dishes are recommended, as plastic dishes tend to become dangerous chew toys.

Have everything ready for your new Bichon before he gets home, and try not to make any sudden changes in his diet.

KENNELING

It is not cruel to place a puppy or dog in a safe kennel or crate. A dog likes to know that he can go to his own special place and get away from the hustle and bustle of the household; they may need a rest from playing children, other humans, or even fellow pets. Placing your dog in his own kennel also allows you to get a rest, to clean the house without worrying about muddy pawprints (at least for

A kennel should never be used as punishment, but rather as a special place where your puppy can rest and be comfortable.

a little while), and to entertain guests who are uncomfortable around a strange dog (believe it or not some people are afraid of dogs!). Kenneling a dog is an excellent "time-out" for both owner and dog and should not be viewed as punishment.

Placing the kennel in a temperature-controlled and well-ventilated area for a few hours at a time is an excellent idea. If you need to leave the puppy during work hours, you should locate a place in the house that is completely safe for the puppy to be alone. Make sure that there are no electrical cords to chew and no lamps or other things to knock over. Leaving a puppy in the bathroom is not advisable, unless you leave the lid on the toilet down and protect the linens.

Try to make your Bichon's arrival as comfortable as possible, and have a place set up that he can call his own.

Placing the kennel in the laundry room is a good idea. Leave the kennel door open, put washable towels inside, and put newspapers on the floor outside of the kennel door. Also leave a dish with fresh water and some safe toys. In doing this you will enjoy your puppy a whole lot more than if you give him free roam of the house. Puppies will have accidents—daily. We left our first puppy in the kitchen one day and came home to chewed cabinets, chairs, and table legs. The scariest part, though, was that the door frame, with the wall telephone cord stapled to it, had been

Ch. PJ's "T" for Two of Keystone CD plays ball. Owner, Patricia Reuter.

chewed in half and the cord was missing. We were later told that had the phone rung while the puppy was chewing that cord, he would have been electrocuted.

Kenneling is not confined merely to times when you are not home. You must determine which rooms of your home you will allow your puppy to go in while he is being supervised. Remember that a puppy does not understand that a carpeted floor is any different from a linoleum or tile floor. Unattended stains can cause serious odor problems and invite revisits. Cleaning the wet or soiled area with

Baby gates are a great way to keep your mischievous puppy out of dangerous areas. Owner, Anne Jones.

a mixture of ammonia and water may discourage future accidents—in that spot. Frequent visits outside are a must for

Frequent visits outside are a must for a puppy, until he learns to recognize his own needs.

puppy, until he learns to recognize his own needs. With maturity usually comes reliability.

It is advisable to go ahead and get a kennel or crate large enough for an adult Bichon. If you select an airline crate, a 200 size is adequate, which is the next to the smallest size. If you live in a warm climate and want a wire crate that allows more air circulation, you may be able to find one at a pet store or you may ask the breeder to obtain one for you through dog shows or other catalog sales. An approximate measurement would be 18 inches wide, 18 inches tall and 24 inches deep. There are also 4 by 4 feet wire puppy pens that have wire flooring. This allows the puppy to have an accident, which will fall to the newspaper-covered

A high-quality, nylon harness and lead set is one of the safest and most secure means of tethering your dog. Photo courtesy of Hagen.

*Providing safe toys will keep your Bichon puppy entertained for hours.
Owner, Karen Pecker.*

flooring below, and the puppy will not have to stand in it. This is the type I prefer, and I feel comfortable about leaving one or two Bichons in this kind of crate all day long while I'm away from home.

This pen also has a removable top that contains the climbing puppy, as well as a gate opening on the side.

TOYS

While at the pet

store, you can also pick up a few safe toys, a lead for future training, grooming scissors, a pin brush and a slicker brush, and a stainless steel comb with a wide and narrow end. Be sure to use a slicker brush that will not damage your puppy's coat. Again, your breeder can help you with these items.

Safe toys should be discussed here. Puppy teeth can tear up many tough-looking things, such as squeaky rubber latex toys, in which case not only is the rubber eaten, but the squeaky goes down too! A Nylabone™, a

An old shoe is NOT a safe chew toy for your Bichon Frise.

soft cloth stuffed toy, or a Nylaball or Gumaball make good toys. The protein in rawhide toys becomes gummy when wet, and adheres to and slowly dissolves the facial hair. A better snack and reward for your Bichon are the small size doggy treats, which you can purchase in your grocery store.

FEEDING

Your breeder will give you feeding instructions, care suggestions, and answers to hypothetical questions. Follow this advice! On a suggestion, I fed my ten-week-old puppies three times per day: morning, late afternoon, and right before bedtime. This last meal of the day was usually a lighter one consisting of a little milk and kibble. As they reached four

Nylabone™ makes a variety of healthy chew toys, such as this Pooch Pacifier, available at your local pet store.

Dolores Wolske's Bichon is all tucked in and ready for dreamland after a nighttime meal.

to five months, I dropped the late afternoon feeding. My reason for this schedule was simply that it fit my lifestyle best. I feed adults one time a day in the morning. Some Bichons have a tendency to gain excess weight and feeding in the morning gave them the whole day to run off the calories. It also made for cleaner nights, as dogs have a very simple digestive system—when something goes in, something must come out. Feeding in the morning and

Bichon puppies love to explore the outdoors together. Owner, Jean Glass.

immediately exercising outdoors usually eliminates any in-house cleanup. Feeding the puppies right before they go to bed helps them to sleep through the night.

TAKING THE PUPPY OUTSIDE

It is preferable to have a fenced-in yard for a dog to grow up in. The fence should be secure enough so that the pup cannot escape, dig out, climb over, or wiggle through, as well as secure enough to prevent other dogs from coming inside it. Dogs are not born with street smarts, and an oncoming vehicle, in their mind, is not an obstacle in their path. Until a dog is taught to "come," to return to you when called, he may think that he has better business on the other side of the street. If your yard is fenced-in there is a swinging two-way door that allows your Bichon to let himself in and out at will. This dog door can be in the exterior

Remember, your Bichon was not born with "street smarts" and should not be free to roam outside until he is properly trained.

wall of your house or in the outside door. There are even dog doors for sliding glass doors. You can lock the door to prevent the dog from going in and out at certain times but this may invite serious bangs on the head, as the dog has no way of knowing that he doesn't have his usual exit privileges. Many attempts to run through the door, only to be hurt while trying, will cause your dog to stop using the door altogether. If you are attempting to keep a cat in, this is not an

Ch. Tomaura Shevaun of Snowberry. Owner, Robert Kendall.

When your Bichon puppy is outside you must keep an eye on him and make sure he doesn't eat any poisonous plants.

Housebreaking is easy if you have a secured yard. Ch. Tomaura's Sky's The Limit.

If drilling a hole in the back of your home doesn't appeal to you, then the advantages of a fenced-in yard are even more important. Letting your Bichon run free in the safety of your yard is a wonderful convenience.

If you are an apartment or townhouse dweller, you have no choice but to walk your puppy. This can quickly become an annoyance, as a puppy usually needs to go out either when it is raining or when you are running late. Housebreaking a pup usually takes longer, too, since you don't have the hurried advantage of opening

option you can use, unless you can keep the cat away from the door, as cats *will* use the door and be thrilled with their freedom to do so.

the back door. You need to think long and hard about pet ownership under these circumstances.

HOUSEBREAKING

Routine is a key word in housebreaking. A regular schedule makes it much easier to housebreak a puppy. You can anticipate his usual needs, and if you get him outside in time, he will eventually get

This Bichon puppy is doing a great job of guarding his two Akita pals. Owner, Daniel DelaRosa.

the message. When a puppy sleeps, he immediately has to urinate upon awakening— sometimes so quickly that picking him up and rushing him out is the only way to prevent an accident.

Be in tune with his personal habits and you can gradually work him into a schedule convenient for you.

OTHER THINGS TO CONSIDER

Are you going to

A Bichon who is allowed to jump on the furniture as a pup will continue to do so as an adult. Set the rules early in your Bichon's life and be consistent.

allow the puppy to jump on the furniture? sleep on the beds? One family member cannot say yes to questions such as these if other family members are saying no. As in child-raising, a unified approach is the only way to get satisfactory results. While the dog is little, attempting to jump up on furniture, your lap, your guests, or your kitchen cabinet may not be a problem and may even be cute. However, once he is grown he will still think that it is okay to do these things and you may have some serious training ahead of you. *It is much easier to set patterns than it*

He may be cute, but he's no angel! An undisciplined puppy will become an unmanageable adult.

is to change implanted habits. The same is true with barking. A little puppy's yip is unimpressive but a

Bichons behind bars! Ch. Tomaura Shevaun of Snowberry, Ch. Snowberry Snob Appeal, and Ch. Sumarco Aloofee Ms. Snowberry.

constant adult bark is annoying and disturbing and may even invite warranted complaints from neighbors. Nip that yip immediately! A puppy that has not been trained good manners will not suddenly have them at two years of age.

Also keep in mind that the Bichon is not an outside breed and if arrangements cannot be made to keep your pet inside, except for regular exercise times, then another breed should be selected.

The Bichon enjoys the cooler weather and despises hot days. Air-conditioning is a must for the hot summer days, especially in the southern states.

THE PUPPY'S FIRST NIGHT

When you bring your new puppy home, the first night will likely be uncomfortable for him as well as for you. Steel your heart against picking up the pitiful, crying puppy who can't understand what happened to the warmth and security of his litter mates and

A Bichon puppy makes two new friends.

Close your ears to your puppy's cries his first few nights home—he will eventually adapt and sleep quietly through the night.

mother. And it may not be just one night—this could go off and on for weeks. *Do not give in to your compassion and go to him.* If you have made sure that there is nothing he can hurt himself on, then try to close your ears and heart to his attempts to get your attention. It is much easier to set a puppy pattern in the beginning than it

A game of tug o' war is a fun time for both master and the playful Bichon.

Two Bichon puppy pals enjoy play time together.

is to change a dominating, determined dog. If you take a sock that you have worn that day and tie a knot in the middle of it and place it in the puppy's bed at night, it will appease him. However, this doesn't always work. I've even heard of people putting a loud ticking clock in the room with the puppy to cover the silence! Don't give in, as you will be sorry later when you are trying to sleep with a playing puppy making noisy demands.

Ch. Tomaura Shevaun of Snowberry as a puppy exploring a new terrain.

Mirror, mirror on the wall, who's the most beautiful Bichon of all?

Grooming

Along with potty training and food scheduling, you should set aside time regularly for grooming. There may not be much coat on your new puppy—but just wait! There is a ton of fluff just waiting to pop out and make your Bichon the glorious animal he is meant to be.

Does your Bichon have a long, thin, straight coat or a thicker, more dense coat? Way back in Bichon history, we determined that the more open, longer coats, which were usually icy-white, came from the French lines and the thicker, curlier, more cottony coats, which appear a bit creamy, were from the Belgian lines. The lines have become so diluted that it is a difficult assumption to make now. Either coat must be treated similarly. The fine coat will develop slower and later in life and usually, with regular care, will not mat as quickly but it generally offers the longer facial, ear, and tail furnishings. The curlier, denser coat is more durable and can take more abuse but is quick to mat.

S. 1/93

The end result of a good grooming session. Ch. Parfait Vision of Love, owned by Joanne Spilman.

However, a six-month-old puppy may have a very plush, showable coat. Grooming this type of coat is pleasurable, as you can sculpt it easily, but by the next day it is showing curls again. No matter which type of coat your Bichon has, they both require care.

PUPPY GROOMING

From the day you select the puppy you must start a maintenance program of coat cultivation. Running the brush and comb through the puppy's coat daily may seem pointless since there is so little, but this training in patience will pay off later.

At about six-months of age, you begin to notice that you have more puppy than you do coat. The undercoat will come

with maturity and the coat will begin to stand out on its own. As you brush your puppy, train him to lie quietly on his side. This is the only way to maintain the

Maintenance of your Bichon's coat begins during puppyhood. Ch. Brereton's Happy Hour.

Brushing and combing your Bichon puppy daily may not seem necessary, but this training in patience will pay off in the future.

luxurious adult coat, which needs to be brushed and combed at least once a week and bathed every three to four weeks.

Every other week, snip the toenails to keep the quick receded. At eight to ten weeks give the puppy a severe trim. Don't touch the tail, ears, or facial whiskers/beard. Unless the back of the neck, called the "mane," is parting or laying down, don't get too drastic with the scissors, but do trim it noticeably and regularly.

BRUSHING

There's a right way and then there's just no other way. *Every* hair must be brushed and not just the ones you can reach without disturbing the dog. Make sure you choose a brush that leaves all of the coat attached. However, a harsher brush may be used for badly matted areas on a coat that is not being prepared for show.

Lying the Bichon on his side, pick up a foot. Hold the toes in the fingers of your left hand (for right-handed people) and hold your slicker brush upward. Always hold the slicker brush upward toward the top of the dog or toward his head. Start

At about 6 months of age, your Bichon may be more puppy than coat, but as he matures, the coat will begin to stand out on its own. Owner, Becky Daniels.

Ch. Tomaura's Bear Fax O' Achlyne.

at a "starting place," such as the top of the leg, and work down. Starting in the middle is not very efficient and it will seem like an eternity to complete the brushing. For the body, grasp in your left hand a wad of coat as wide as you can comfortably control. With the full length of your thumb being the controller, release a "row" of hair as you are brushing

Ch. Jalwi Pattern of Pawmark. Owned by the author.

from the base of the roots outward. Please note that I did not say "brush from the skin." Brush that row, then release another row or section and continue brushing upward. Continue to move your left hand up, away from the brushing action. All of the coat below your brush will be thoroughly mat-free and the coat above your brush and in your left hand is your

This little Bichon is as pretty as a princess. Owner, Ann Freeman.

destination. This is the *only* way you will ever have a completely brushed, mat-free Bichon. If this is not clear, try and visualize a row of hair about to be rolled in a small curler. You basically have to section this hair off in order to get a grip on it. After you have gone over an area of the dog with the brush, take the wide end of the comb and go over him again. Certain areas may require the narrow end but only after you are sure there are no more mats. Those narrow teeth hurt quite a bit when they hit a tangle. Do not touch the tail or beard with a slicker. Instead, use

A Bichon pup in her Sunday best.

a pin brush and repeat the same procedure of releasing a segment of hair as above. If there is a mat there, try to peel it apart with your fingers, pin brush it,

White-coated breeds such as the Bichon require special care because they show dirt quickly and stain easily.

and then comb it. If it is still there, you may have to use the slicker gently. Remember, your goal is to save and cultivate the coat.

A white-coated breed requires special care. They show dirt quickly and stain easily and, if long-coated as is the Bichon, Lhasa Apso or Maltese, require brushing and bathing every three to four weeks. The coat on the feet of a white dog are in constant contact with dirt and if that dirt is black soil, their feet become black or if, in the case of the south where the dirt has a reddish tint, the feet can turn pink, brown, and even red. The same is true for the face when the eyes weep. The dampness of the tears constantly running down the face turns the coat a dirty color that will not wash out. There are several

Grooming the Bichon is not a simple task, but the job is made easier with the right equipment.

For quick trims cordless grooming devices are available at your local pet shop. Photo courtesy of Wahl Clipper.

causing an irritation; blocked tear ducts, resulting from teething, a bad cold, unclean ears, or an eye infection; incorrectly placed eyelashes, which need to be treated or removed by a veterinarian; and/or a constant glare from the sun, causing need to continuously bathe the eyeball. Sometimes a puppy's tear ducts have not grown rapidly enough to take care of the flow of tears, thus allowing the ducts to get stopped up and tearing to begin. If you make a daily conscientious effort to remove all residue from around the eyes, groom the coat so no

reasons for tear staining: wisps of hair constantly in the eye,

Ch. Dove Cote's Mr. Magoo shows off his beautifully groomed head.

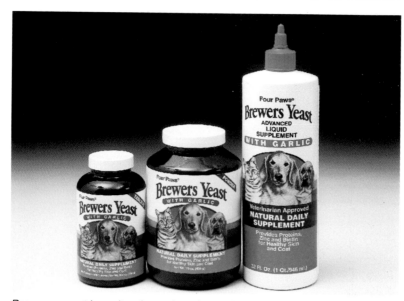

Brewers yeast has vitamins, minerals, and proteins that can enhance your Bichon's coat and help control shedding. Photo courtesy of Four Paws.

hair touches the eyeball, and treat all infections and ailments promptly, you should have no problems with tear staining.

BATHING

Now that your Bichon is mat-free, he is ready for a bath and a trim. If you want to dull your scissors almost as quickly as if you rubbed them on a block of concrete, scissor a dirty Bichon coat. If you want a

Ch. Sandcastle Bikini, owned by Linda Dickens.

smooth even trim, bathe and blow dry your Bichon completely before trimming. Before you put him in the sink, pull the hair from the ears. An easy way of doing this is with hemostats. Pull a little

Since the Bichon Frise is prone to tear staining, you may want to use a product that is made specifically for this problem. Photo courtesy of Four Paws.

at a time, but be quick. Remember, the ear canal is not the Grand Canyon and you can only go in the clearly visible apron of the ear. This isn't the most comfortable thing a dog must endure but it is for his health. Also, clean the hair out of the pads with scissors or at least cut it flush with the pads. Debris loves to collect in the long hair of the foot, causing all sorts of problems. If you haven't clipped the toenails, do that now also.

Please remember that when you are using the comb and you hit a snag, yanking on it or forcing the teeth of

Clip your Bichon's toenails at least once every two weeks to keep the quick receded. Photo by Vince Serbin.

the comb through the tangle hurts.

Before you pick up the puppy for bathing

you should have a couple of towels available, the shampoo mixed with the appropriate amount of warm water, and the dryer, brush, and comb handy. You will need a non-slippery table to work on at a comfortable height for you. You can "make do" with a cardtable with towels affixed to the top of it and a chair for you to sit. You will need to be near an electrical outlet for the dryer.

I prefer a shampoo without any whitening agents in it for routine, non-show bathing, as I feel the optical brighteners tend to dry the coat. However, if the coat has become a bit dull from summer insect repellents or winter gas heat, you can use

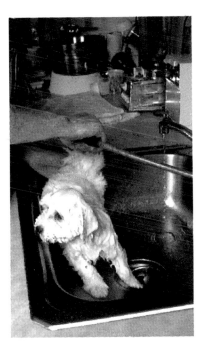

Facing Page: *A well-groomed Bichon, Ch. Parfait Vision of Love.* Right: *When bathing your Bichon, never stop up the sink. Bichons do not like to stand in water and will become frightened.*

a green or blue shampoo, as these usually contain whitening products. You will probably have to bathe your Bichon for several weeks to successfully lift the discoloring.

However, if you are doing routine bathing you will need a deep sink with a spray-type nozzle and a good bit of force to allow you to correctly clean your dog. *Never stop up the sink.* For the most part, dogs do not like to stand in water.

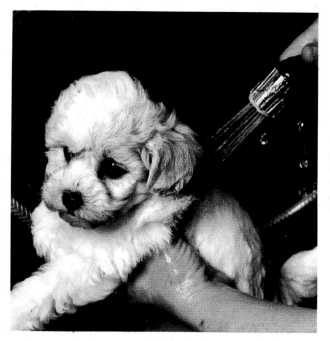

A deep sink with a spray nozzle is perfect for routine bathing of your Bichon Frise.

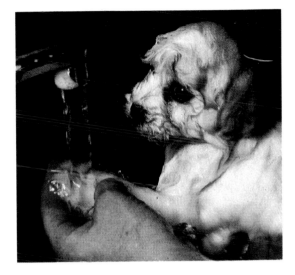

Thoroughly clean your Bichon's paws, as dirt has a tendency to build up in the long hair of the foot.

Swimming in the old swimming hole is one thing but this contrived pool of water is a threat.

Lifting the head slightly to allow the water to run away from the nose, with your left hand under the chin, move the spray of warm water to the top of the head and begin wetting down the coat. Your dog will automatically close his eyes, even if he is a puppy. He may be jumping, screaming, and lurching, but his eyes will be shut. Keeping the ear flaps down, as you *never* want to get water in the ears, wet the ear hair. Bring the

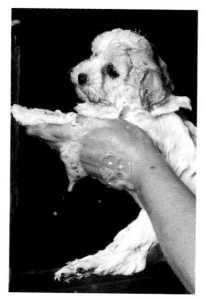

When lathering your Bichon, knead the coat like dough, squeezing the suds thoroughly through each strand of hair.

careful not to get water on, near, up, over, under, or through the nose. Once your dog thinks he's drowning, panic will set in. Move the spray down the front legs, etc., until the entire dog is thoroughly wet from front to back, top to bottom. Be cautious not to move the spray nozzle in a circular motion. If you hold the spray a couple of inches away from the hair you will get a better rinse. Expose the anal glands and rinse before you apply the shampoo.

hose around to one side of the muzzle and soak it, then move it off of the face and around *far in front of the nose* and wet the other side of the muzzle. *Be extremely*

Left hand under the chin again, have the shampoo mixture ready and thin enough to pour through the narrow opening of any kind of plastic bottle with a flip-up pouring spout. Squeeze the shampoo on the top of the head, the cheeks, and the beard on both sides, avoiding the eyes at all cost. If you saturate the beard, there is no need to pour shampoo directly toward the mouth. Proceed to squeeze the remainder of the shampoo mixture over the rest of the dog.

The Bichon coat will dry curly if left to dry on its own, so speed is vital in the drying process.

The underside of the dog must be washed, also. You will use about $1\frac{1}{2}$ to 2 cups of shampoo mixture at each bathing.

If you are trying to whiten a dull winter coat, the best process is to soap the coat thoroughly with a whitening product and lather until any natural shampoo color is gone and you only have white suds all over the dog. Leave the shampoo on for about five minutes, then rinse.

This is what your Bichon should look like when you properly comb, brush, and dry: straight hair with no curls.

If you lather and rub the coat in circular motions, you are tying each and every hair on the dog's body in an unforgiving knot. A better way is to knead the coat like dough—squeezing the suds thoroughly through each strand of hair, thus cleaning it to the best of your ability. Slide some of the suds to the underside of the chest, the stomach, and the inside of the back legs. Once he is sufficiently soaped and gone over with your hands, you may begin to rinse.

A finishing rinse will aid in keeping your Bichon's coat from curling. Photo courtesy of Hagen.

RINSING

This is the most vital part of bathing a dog, in my opinion.

Fail here and the ultimate disaster will discourage you from trying to clean your dog yourself ever again—not to mention that soap left on the coat and skin causes an itch that requires scratching, which rips the coat out, makes

A sturdy table with a grooming post will make grooming sessions with your Bichon a breeze.

sores, and cannot be remedied by ointment. If you must time yourself, then plan on ten to fifteen minutes for rinsing. Turn the spray nozzle upside down to thoroughly get the underside, "armpits," belly, inside of all legs, etc. You will soon get the hang of doing this without spraying water right in your face! Rinse, rinse, and then rinse for another five minutes.

Squeeze what water you can from the coat,

Ch. Miri-Cals Shenanigans licks her nose clean. Owner, Miriam Barnharl

then, with a towel between your hand and the dog's coat, squeeze or rather press the water from the entire coat again. Discard that towel and start again with a dry towel. Your Bichon is now ready to be moved from the sink to the grooming table.

With a large pin brush, brush/comb *gently* through the coat to straighten as much of the curl as possible and to remove any tangles caused by the bath

Brush gently through the coat to straighten the curl and to remove tangles.

and/or the towels.
You might check the
ears for dampness
and gently dry them
with cotton wrapped
around the end of
forceps or use a
cotton swab. If too
much water is in
there, a little alcohol
on the cotton will
quickly dry it. Don't
gouge and poke
around in the ear.

BLOWING DRY

If you are using
your own hair dryer
rather than a
professional dog
dryer, you must put
the setting on *low* or
else you will burn your
Bichon's skin horribly.
Do not point the dryer
closer than 10 inches
from the dog. The
higher the velocity the

*This Bichon is looking all primped
and proper after a lengthy
grooming session.*

smoother the coat will
be when you are done.

The type of dryer you
are using will
determine your next
step. If it is the "force"
type, all that is
required is a one-
handed procedure.

Am./Can. Ch. Norvic's Easy Does It, ROM. Owner, Robert Kendall.

Since the coat will dry curly if left to dry on its own, speed is vital in the drying process. Start with the face. Some dogs will let you dry their faces with a force dryer and some will not. If your Bichon can't stand all of that air in his face, use the warm air type of dryer and slicker brush for the head and face. With the air blowing from behind the cheek, brush the beard forward and attempt to move the hair towards the underside of the chin, like a pageboy hairdo. Next do the topknot and ears. However, the ears are the least of your priorities at this point, as they don't tend to curl so easily. Remember, you are fighting the natural drying time and you want to get to every inch of the coat before it dries by itself.

If you don't thoroughly dry as you go along, the curl will return immediately. Unfortunately, mats will set in a damp coat and in all of the hard-to-reach places. Be sure the area you are working on is completely dry before moving on to the next. Always brush toward the head—legs up, body forward, mane up, and tail out and up. On the face and tail, to preserve hair, use a pin brush 90 percent of the time. There are a few times when the slicker becomes necessary.

If you are using the force dryer on the dog, he will stand the entire time. If you are

Brush the beard forward and attempt to move the hair toward the underside of chin.

using a warm air dryer, you may lie him on his side, blow the hair toward the head, and brush where the air separates the coat, continuously moving the air upward upon completely drying each section—just like the brushing techniques.

Everything must be blown and/or blown and brushed. After the dog has been gone over with air and/or brush and air, go over him again one more time. Turn off the dryer and watch your Bichon take a deep sigh and relax! Stand him up, take your

Always brush toward the head —legs up, body forward, mane up, and tail out and up.

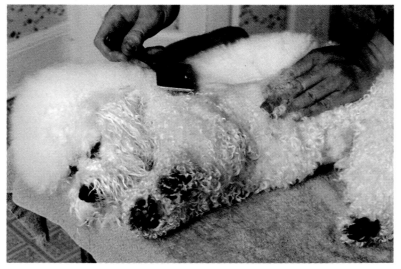

Your Bichon must be completely dry before you begin to scissor and trim.

metal comb with the wide end, and carefully go through the coat from head to tail. The force dryer will leave you a few manageable tangles that you must dislodge now. Take your hands and check every inch for dampness—underside too. If you are 110 percent satisfied, you may proceed to scissor your dog.

TRIMMING

If this is not your skill or interest, you

Trimming your Bichon can be tricky. If you have no skill or interest, find a groomer that will trim to your satisfaction.

need to search immediately for a reputable grooming shop that can build a rapport with your Bichon and can satisfy what you want your dog to look like.

You have looked at pictures of properly groomed Bichons and you can show them to the groomer if he is unfamiliar with the breed. Many groomers attempt to make Bichons look like Poodles. They indent the coat above the ears and cut the body and legs all the same, overly short length. The Bichon head is a picture of roundness, as are the legs. The coat on the sides of the face and under the ears is never cut—it is only shaped a very small bit on the bottom to give it the rounded look. The coat over the eyes is left longer than a Poodle, in an "awning" effect. The body can be kept shorter, but the coat on the top side of the neck, the "mane", should be kept longer.

SKIN PROBLEMS

White-coated dogs seem to be prone to

A well-groomed Bichon is a happy Bichon! Photo by Isabelle Francais.

skin problems. Dogs of all colors and breeds have a high sensitivity to fleas and develop skin lesions that are so severe that they require veterinarian care. Many Bichons have this problem. Outdoor cats, who are a great host to the flea, and Bichons are not compatible, only because of the flea allergy and not because they do not get along. Bichons get

Since Bichons are highly sensitive to fleas, they should not be exposed to outdoor cats.

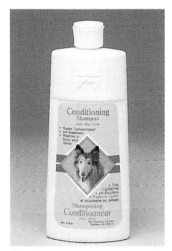

A good conditioning shampoo, like this one from Hagen, is ideal for the Bichon's white fluffy coat.

infestation, you must not only treat the animal but must spray the house and yard every two weeks. Keeping everything clean discourages this minute pest. There are several products available that are not

Miri-Cals Arabella. Owner, Carol Haines.

along with anyone and anything. A protein-rich diet encourages skin eruptions. A dirty coat is a breeding ground for skin irritations and makes a Bichon very uncomfortable.

To prevent a flea

very chemically strong and rely mostly on natural properties to repel parasites. Check with your local pet supply store or attend a local dog show and shop at the many booths that carry more pet supplies than most local stores. This is also a good time to talk with breeders of not only Bichons but other coated breeds and find out what their flea program is.

The Bichon head is a picture of roundness, as are the legs. Photo by Robert Pearcy.

Taking a few precautions to prevent fleas and ticks will ensure the outdoor happiness of your Bichon Frise.

Ch. Chaminade Improvisation, owned by Michael and Terry Ravin.

The Growing Bichon

Watching your puppy grow is wonderful! It's as if he changes right before your very eyes, but on the other hand, he looks the same. At about five to six months of age there will be more dog than coat as he goes through the lanky, awkward teen period. Then suddenly the undercoat will start coming in and the brushing routine you have established will really pay off.

At about four or five

Your Bichon puppy will go through a lanky, awkward period around 5-6 months of age.

months of age your puppy will start losing his baby teeth. If he eats them, it's O.K. You must pay close attention to his bite before this age. If his mouth looks like it may not turn out to be a scissors bite, you can pull certain teeth a bit early, as nature will fill the gap quickly and those new teeth will act as a brace for the rest of the teeth. In other words, if your puppy is undershot (bottom teeth in front of top teeth in a

Certain teeth may be pulled from a puppy's mouth to attain an adult scissor bite.

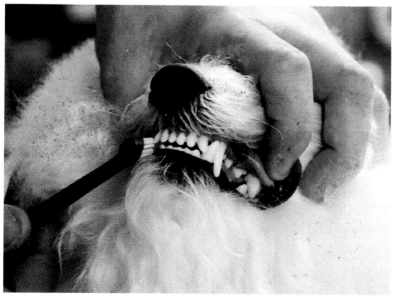

It is a joy to watch your Bichon grow through various puppy stages and into adulthood.

bulldog fashion), you would want to pull the top front teeth early to hold the bottom ones back when they come in later. Watching your puppy's mouth is very valuable, as the tissue of the gums is an excellent health indicator.

Bichons are definitely lap dogs and, in my opinion, should be allowed this closeness. Their purpose in life is to be good companions and

The Bichon Frise is definitely a lap dog. Ch. Norvic's Simply Smashing, owned by Robert Kendall.

good friends.

As your pet becomes older and housebreaking has become fairly successful, he can be allowed more and more freedom and everyone can relax a bit. But discipline must not be ignored. If you did not permit him to bark when he was a puppy, he probably won't as an adult. He may decide at some mature date to start responding to sounds he hears. It is very important that you stop him immediately with "Bad dog!" A couple of announcement barks when someone comes to the door can be helpful, but continued yapping is unpleasant.

At approximately six months of age your puppy will be eating one meal a day, providing he is a good weight. If he is very active, he may burn more calories than he should and he will need plenty of food for those growing spurts.

A Bichon who is disciplined for barking as a pup probably will not bark as an adult.

At about this same age he will go through the rather unattractive gangly period. Never fear—he will come back to being the round ball of fluff that attracted your eye in the beginning, just bigger.

You will get your puppy's immunization record from the breeder when you pick him up. I recommend that the puppy be taken to your veterinarian within 24 hours of purchase. Let the vet check out and verify that your puppy is sound. He can then put the puppy's health record on the chart and will advise you when to bring

Your Bichon will go through an ugly, gangly stage before becoming a full grown version of the round ball of fluff that originally attracted your eye.

Can you find the Bichon Frise in this picture? Owner, Ann Freeman.

your pet back in for his adult shots. Do not put off this important step in protecting your puppy. Developing a good rapport with your vet is very important to you and your Bichon.

Bichons enjoy learning tricks. The family member who takes delight in and has the patience for teaching the dog will develop a great relationship with him. Playing tug of war with an old sock, if

Bichons love to play and learn tricks. Tossing a ball for a game of fetch is a fun first lesson for you and your Bichon.

done gently, can help loosen the baby teeth. Throwing a soft toy for a lesson in retrieve/ fetch is excellent training for future necessary commands.

Ch. Gaylor's Mr. Magic of Glenelfred caught kissing Krista Fileccia. Owner, Gail Antetomaso.

An agile Bichon Frise flies over a hurdle.

Training

As my puppies get a little older (two to three months), but are still willing to let me dominate, I take them into my front yard without a leash and begin giving them the voice command "Stay with me!," and I accompany my command with physical action telling them what they are

Puppies are especially eager to learn new tricks. Photo by Isabelle Francais.

A show lead is highly recommended when walking your Bichon. Most collars and leashes are too rough on the Bichon's fragile mane.

supposed to be doing. When they can walk to the mailbox with me without a leash, stay out of the street, and return upon command, I will feel very secure that should the day come when they accidentally get out, they have a good chance of knowing what to do.

It is not advisable to put a permanent collar on a Bichon as this will rub the coat around the neck and you will never develop the "mane", which is so important to the arch of the neck. Using a flea collar is definitely not recommended for the health of your Bichon. A show lead made of a thin braid of twine,

This Bichon is taking the baby for a walk. Owner, Ann Freeman.

purchased at the pet supply or dog show, can be used when you want to take your puppy for a walk. A leash is a two-piece apparatus involving a collar and a leash for you to hold. This has always seemed too much trouble to me, but some people prefer this method.

Teaching a Bichon to walk on a lead, if done easily and with fun in mind, should be a joy and not a dismal affair. Put the lead around his neck and push the catch up to about $\frac{1}{2}$ an inch to 1 inch from his neck. Let him drag it around the house for a while to get used to the feeling. Go to the kitchen and get some treats to slip in your pocket. When it is time to go outside, pick him up and put him down where you wish to begin the walk. Trying

Teaching your Bichon to walk on a lead should be enjoyable for both dog and master. Ch. Dove Cote's Joy from Heaven.

Allowing your Bichon to drive the family car will increase his self-confidence and give him a wonderful feeling of independence.

Take a deep breath.... Eileen training "Wonder Dog," a Bichon Frise rescue dog owned by Chester Kurowski of Marlboro, New Jersey.

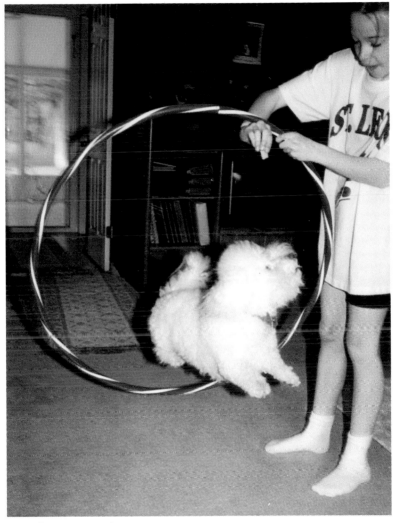

....and away we go!

Hurdling is just as exciting and fun for the Bichon as it is for the spectator.

to teach him to follow you through the door, down the steps, and around the car is just more than he can take in at first. Once you are outside and ready for the walk, holding the lead loosely in your hand, take a small step and encourage him to come with you. After he's taken several steps, either following you or with you, give him a treat and tell him what a good boy he is. Praise is very important when he accomplishes anything that you want him to do. How else is he going to know that he is doing the right thing if you don't affirm his actions? Don't panic if he squeals and acts as if he is being killed! He's not—he's merely asserting his stubbornness and you're being Alpha (dominant) in his life.

Bang! You're dead! Photo courtesy of Chester Kurowski.

This atmosphere must be established early and maintained his entire life. *You are the boss*, but not bossy. This is extremely important. Kindness

Given an ample reward, your Bichon can learn to do almost anything.

with consistent firmness will get you further than harshness. Bichons will love you no matter what you do, therefore you must be extremely careful not to abuse that trust.

Keep your leadbreaking lessons to a brief five to ten minutes a day, at first. After a week you can increase the lessons to twice a day. Another few weeks and you can increase the time of the lessons. Don't rush—you have his entire lifetime. Always hold the lead in your left hand with the puppy on your left side at all times. This leaves your right hand free. Never walk your dog on hot asphalt in

What better reward for a job well done than a chicken-flavored Nylabone™?

the summertime. Slip your shoe off: if the ground, concrete, or asphalt is uncomfortable for you, you can be assured it will be for him. If you are a runner, it really isn't advisable to ask your dog to run a mile with you. Be sure you have fresh water waiting at home after each outing. You

Teach your Bichon to "come" before you allow him to roam around without a lead.

for bite, but this is something you do not want to encourage in any dog. If another dog should be loose on the street and run up to your puppy, pick your puppy up immediately and either "shoo" the other dog away or return home. Please understand that I am not condoning a weak, sissy dog—I am just extremely opposed to

Through proper training and conditioning, your Bichon Frise will prove to be a surprisingly agile athlete.

Your Bichon puppy will grow up to be an even more enjoyable companion as an adult.

aggressive dogs and feel that they have no place in the world. An attack-trained dog has his place but not in the passive comfort of my home.

As your puppy becomes an adult, enjoy his antics, companionship, love, and dependency. When he reaches his mature years of twelve years or greater, his needs may change. He will become more sedentary and require less exercise. However, he must have the same amount, if not more, of your love and carc.

The time you sharc with a Bichon Frise is all quality time and is very rewarding. When you are sad, there is nothing more comforting than the concerned eyes of your little companion wishing to help you. Thcy rcjoicc and jump

The soft, concerned eyes of your Bichon Frise will lift you up on your grayest days.

Your Bichon Frise will provide you with unconditional love and companionship through every stage of his life.

for joy when you are happy and that is a bonding emotion also. Just remember to reward your little pal with a rub under the chin, a scratch on the tummy, and many kind words. You can't buy that kind of love, at any price.

The Bichon Frise is a sensitive breed that will mirror the emotions of its master.

The author awarding Best of Breed at a dog show.

Showing Your Dog

There are shows, and then there are shows.

All-breed shows and trials offer a bit of everything. Each entry is a purebred dog of a recognized breed, and at all-breed shows, there may be as many as 130 or more breeds entered. Trials are for obedience competition and may be held in conjunction with breed shows. Specialty shows are for one breed only, and

You can enter your Bichon Frise in any of a variety of competitions at both all-breed and specialty shows.

The winners of the Breeder of the Year competition at the 1991 Specialty.

national specialties are hosted by the national "parent" club, usually accompanied by a great deal of hoopla.

Field trials, tracking tests, hunting tests, herding tests and trials and other instinct tests are usually held outdoors and are often hosted separately. Instinct, agility and temperament tests are offered as added attractions more and more frequently at large all-breed and national shows.

At one time, all shows were benched with entries tied to their cubicles for spectators to observe. Now, benched shows have declined, and few are still in existence. Every dog lover should attend at least one of these benched events, either as a competitor or spectator. Some exhibitors decorate their benches and spread picnic lunches on grooming tables. Since the dogs are required to stay on their benches for several hours, it's a good opportunity for

A pooped-out Bichon takes a break on the grooming table at a dog show.

Every dog lover should attend at least one bench show to examine the finest examples of each breed.

showing off the breeds, sharing knowledge, making contacts, observing other breeds, talking "dogs" and having a good time. At other exhibitions, it's usually "show and go."

Competitive events are showcases for the breeders' best. Sometimes it's more fun to observe, but

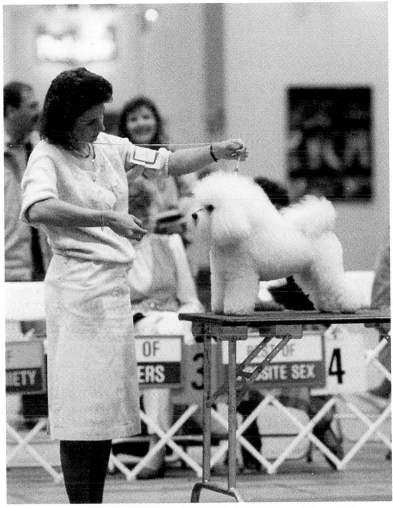

*Ch. Sandcastle Bikini, owned by Linda Dickens, at an all-breed show.
Photo by Michele Perlmutter.*

Competitive shows are the ultimate thrill for breeders who wish to showcase their best Bichons. Photo by Robert Smith.

point. Once that goal is attained, excitement mounts and the drive is on to reach the top in our field: Championship, a Best of Breed, a Group I, a Best in Show, Top-winning Dog; a High in Trial, a 200 score, an OTCh, Super Dog at the Gaines Classic; a field or herding trial placement, an instinct Championship, National Gun Dog Champion.

true enthusiasts will tell you that when they aren't competing, they feel the itch.

As with any other passion, showing is a progressive disease. It starts slowly with a yen to have the dog behave and show well, to be in the placings, to obtain a leg or a

DOG SHOW MANIA

Most first-time buyers have no interest in showing. Oftimes the show bug bites the unsuspecting shortly after joining a training class. Following the initial exposure, the future show addict weakens and the "disease" settles in for a long-term stay and occasionally is terminal.

As the weeks proceed, we note how smart and/or beautiful our dog is compared to the others in the class. When a notice is passed about a nearby match, we decide to enter just for the fun of it. That's why it's called a fun match.

People go and have a

The hubbub of a dog show outdoors. Here the judge is examining a Bichon Frise.

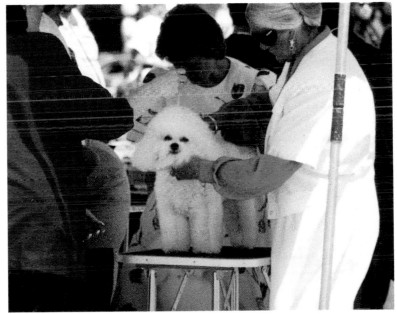

Realtors start calling about the five acres for sale just outside of town.

By this point, the enthusiast is eyeing another dog or three and planning the kennel building with indoor/outdoor runs. Often our first dog

Don't expect your first Bichon to win big at the shows. Just have fun and learn as much as you can for future showing.

does not take the pro world by its ear, and we decide that ol' Phydeaux can enjoy life by the fireside while we set forth to search for the Wonder Pup that stirs the judges' blood.

Depending on our experience and knowledge, we demand *top show quality* and qualify this with specifics: showmanship, natural instinct, a gorgeous head, superior movement, intelligence, and so on.

We know what we want—perfection. The trick is obtaining or breeding that ideal . . . or even coming close to it. That's what showing is all about: the quest for the ideal. To reach

Two show-quality Bichons Frises. Photo by Isabelle Francais.

that unreachable star. It's not exactly tilting at windmills, because some come close— close enough to touch the star's tip, to be thrilled by its warmth. But perfection has not yet been attained. No dog scores 200 every time it walks into the obedience ring, and never has one remained unbeaten for its career in the breed ring.

CLUBS

Joining a club is probably the best way

An appreciative Bichon thanks the author for her excellent judgment.

to learn, advance and eventually help others attain their goals. Almost anywhere there are dogs, there is a dog club. More than 3,000 dog clubs exist, and these clubs host approximately 10,000 AKC-sanctioned events annually.

Clubs bring together people interested in a common cause, in this case, their dogs. Whether we want to attain a conformation or obedience title, to breed better animals or simply to enjoy our canine companion, we can do it in the company of others who love dogs.

It's encouraging to have friends cheer us on in our attempts. Tailgate parties are more fun when friends are along, and when several club members attend a show, there's usually someone who has cause to celebrate.

Most clubs hold annual shows,

Bichons and their handlers parading around the show ring. Photo by Robert Smith.

matches and other doggy events such as instinct tests, seminars, demonstrations and training classes. A list of breeders within the club is made available to those searching for puppies or studs.

If you are serious about showing your Bichon, the first thing you should do is join a club.

Most important, a club consists of members. Members who hold our hand when our pal is in surgery, who bring the bubbly when our dog finishes and who offer advice and company during a whelping.

It's having friends who help us through the hard times or who hold an extra dog at ringside. No matter what happens, someone has already walked in our shoes. When we come in fifth out of five, have a pup going through the teenage ganglies or own a bitch who has trouble conceiving, someone can usually console us and either offer advice or supply the name of someone

An appreciative Bichon thanks the author for her excellent judgment.

who can. Being a club member means we can have company who doesn't care about dog hair in the coffee and who comes to visit wearing jeans already marked with paw prints.

Club membership is caravaning to shows, helping to tow another out of a mud-sucking field or jump-starting a battery on a sub-zero day. Members care

Joining a club will benefit both you and your Bichon, as you will make new friends with people who care about dogs as much as you do.

about each other and about their dogs.

TRAINING

Training classes are offered through these organizations and by experienced individuals. Although it's possible to train a dog without attending a class, it's difficult to test an animal's abilities without distractions. With other dogs and people around, our dog may find them more interesting than our commands. But dogs have to learn to behave under any circumstance. Many an owner claims, "I can't understand it.

He's does it all fine at home."

A class instructor knows how to solve a problem when teams are at a stalemate in an exercise and can correct us when we're doing something wrong to lead the dog astray. Besides, group

A Bichon must learn to ignore distractions if he is to succeed in the dog show world.

training is sure more fun than doing it by ourselves.

Training is valuable for all dogs and all owners, not just those who are going into competition. Probably 80 percent of all people who register for a training class simply want a well-behaved companion. The all-important bonding is intensified when dog and master learn to work together and develop respect for one another.

The proper gait is a vital part of Bichon conformation and judging. Photo by Robert Smith.

Signing up for a training class will be a positive experience regardless of whether or not you choose to show your Bichon.

Training doesn't stop with class, however. It continues at home, through practicing the stack, the stay, moving on leash, and through bringing out the best in our dogs by conditioning them.

CONDITIONING

Making sure our dog is in prime condition

Hours and hours of practice are necessary when you enter your Bichon into competitive dog shows.

at all times includes training, exercising, grooming, instilling confidence and seeking veterinary care. Although it's best to begin exposing the dog to various situations by eight weeks, it can be accomplished at older ages if a newcomer to the sport decides to jump in.

Professional breeders begin handling their pups at birth, gently touching, caressing and talking to them. As the pups grow, they are exposed to household noise and activity. No one goes through life tiptoeing about. Dropped pots and slammed doors are a part of our lives and our dogs'.

Nail clipping begins, as a necessity, at one week of age or the dam pays the penalty with painful scratches on her sensitive breasts. Breeders weigh each individual, offering tiny tidbits and loving caresses. Setting pups on tables and gently brushing them is good practice for all dogs, show or pet, and should begin in small doses at five or six weeks. Pups should learn to walk on

various footing—lawns, carpets and linoleum.

When the litter is about six weeks old, leash training can begin with pups following the dam or

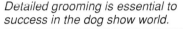
Detailed grooming is essential to success in the dog show world.

walking at will with the owner following them. After a few days of this, the owner can start changing directions, clucking and talking to the pup, encouraging it to follow.

Games such as hide and seek teach the puppies that owners do return, and a little later encourages the dogs to use their noses to find people and objects. Chasing a ball and returning it for more tosses introduces the retrieve.

As soon as the first vaccination is given, acclimation to crates

Your awkward little puppy may someday grow to be a Champion Bichon. Photo by Vince Serbin.

Ch. Tomaura's Mighty Samson and Ch. Tomaura's Delightful Delilah as pups

and traveling can begin, heading for parks, training classes and other fun places, not just the vet clinic. Fun matches offer classes for two-month-old puppies, and sanctioned matches and shows are open to dogs at least six months of age. Even if the puppy isn't ready for serious competition, matches make excellent

who causes a sensation, a murmur in the crowd. The dog who always draws the spectators and surreptitious glances from the judges in the adjoining rings.

It's handling that dog to countless Best of Breed (BOB), Group and Best in Show (BIS) wins, smashing records and setting new ones. And moving around the yard with a youngster who never sets a foot down wrong and knowing . . . just knowing . . . that this is the one that will take you all the way, close enough to snag that star.

We soon learn the jargon and doggy

A regular exercising regimen will physically condition your Bichon for dog show competition. Photo by Robert Smith.

Training for this Bichon is more fun than work. Photo by Robert Smith.

etiquette. Fifteen points make a Champion; nine of these points may be obtained in minor (one or two-point) competition. Two majors (three-to-five points) are required, and at least three judges must have found the dog worthy of receiving points.

Majors are do-or-die occasions. Because majors are almost as

Ch. Parfait Vision of Love. Owner, Joanne Spilman.

scarce as tickets to the World Series and just about as difficult to win, one does not cause that major to break by withdrawing a dog unless one has a death wish.

But all of this starts with a first training class, where the handler and the pup learn to walk, and then run, without tripping over each other. Here the trainer teaches the handlers to bring out the best in

Pat Reuter showing and finishing her Bichon Frise, Ch. Keystone's Rocky of Orlando.

Bichon and handler walk gracefully around the show ring.

their dogs and to look graceful while doing so. Some of us never attain this ability and hire a professional to do the job.

Handlers are convenient. Showing is their job, and they don't have bosses grumbling when they take time off work to attend events. Because they are able to travel and participate in more shows, their dogs win more frequently. Because their dogs win more frequently, they attain more clients. And compete more often, and win more often. And on and on and on.

Breeders often have other commitments besides jobs. There are spouses, "What! You're

A pretty Bichon owned by Estelle and Wendy Kellerman. Photo by Isabelle Francais

going another weekend?" Children, "But, Dad, I wanna go to the beach." And whelping demands, "So you want me to cross my hocks until you come back, or what?"

Because handling is their career, pros have the experience and finesse amateurs often lack. When a person spends 40 hours a week doing something, he or she is usually more competent than

If you would like to show your Bichon, but don't have the time, you may want to consider hiring a professional handler.

those of us who eke out an hour or two of our spare time.

Occasionally, an owner doesn't attend any of the shows but sends the dog off with a professional until the Championship or honors sought are attained. Once the decision is made to hire a pro, we must decide who is the best for our dog. Most handlers specialize within a group or type. For instance, one person may handle all terriers, but nothing else. Another concentrates on "coaty" dogs, such as the Poodle, Bichon Frise and Pomeranian.

Find out who wins consistently at shows and ask other owners for advice. Observe, also, the handler's treatment of her dogs. Does she truly like dogs? Do she and her dogs look like a team when competing? Or is this only a way to earn

This Bichon shows good conformation and a proper tail.

extra money on weekends?

Ask to watch the grooming session. Is he thorough, yet gentle? Do his charges like him? Notice whether he is firm or rough in his methods. Cleanliness of facilities and exercise areas counts too.

Owners should be compatible with their

A good handler will have clean facilities and will handle your Bichon gently during grooming sessions.

dogs' handlers, and so should the animals. If there is a personality clash, someone's going to lose. Most times, it's the dog.

Ascertain the fees before making any verbal or written agreement to hire someone. A few professionals charge a higher fee per show, but cover expenses themselves. Most charge expenses in addition to their fee.

Discuss all financial responsibilities before you hire a professional handler.

You may be able to share expenses if the handler has several other clients, but that usually means sharing time as well. Ask what happens when she has a conflict in another ring. Some handlers have assistants or work out reciprocal agreements with other pros.

Discuss all possibilities in advance: veterinary care, bonuses for special wins, splitting of cash awards, length of commitment, and so

A professional handler will keep you updated on your Bichon's performance.

on. Even if you send your dog with the handler for a period of time, she should call regularly to let you know how he's doing and to work out further details. That's the meaning of—and the reason for—a professional.

Everyone has different methods of obtaining goals. With some, the game is incomplete unless they themselves breed, train and exhibit their dogs. Others are content with buying a superstar and cheering from the sidelines. Still others fall somewhere in between. Whatever the route, the final destination is the same, to own a dog that excites the senses—and the judge.

For many exhibitors, the challenge lies at specialty shows. Winning under a judge who has a depth of knowledge about—and perhaps has bred, owned and/or exhibited—this particular breed is a coup. particularly when the win is over a large number of other quality entries. Gaining the nod at a national specialty show is especially gratifying. There will always be a thrill at being chosen the best among one's peers.

Most people compete at all-breed shows frequently, however, possibly because there are more of these events than specialties. Here the excitement mounts as each hurdle is met and overcome: the class win, Winners, Breed, Group and ultimately BIS. These

Breeding the perfect Bichon is an inexact science.

achievements feed the progressive urge to conquer.

OBEDIENCE

Many owners sign up for a training class, hoping the results will give them a well-behaved pet. At discovering the yet untapped intelligence of our dogs, we yearn to find out just how good they really are.

For many owners, the goal is to gain titles (Companion Dog, CD; Companion Dog Excellent, CDX; Utility Dog, UD) which proclaim their pets' ability and their own prowess in training.

The Bichon Frise is exhibited in the Non-Sporting Group at all-breed shows.

Tres Beau N'Est Ce Pas, owned by Linda Dickens and Clayt Arnold. Photo by Tom Dickens.

Three passes (or legs) under three judges, and that's enough.

But a few hone the competitive edge, going for an Obedience Trial Championship (OTCh), as well as top wins in individual breeds and in all-breeds. To win an OTCh, the dog must garner 100

Bichons and their handlers pose for the judge.

points from winning first or second placings in Open and Utility Classes against all breeds, including those who already have their OTCh. Capturing High in Trial (HIT), whether at an all-breed, specialty or national show, is a coup that all serious competitors seek.

Special trials such as the Windsor Classic, the Gaines Regionals and Classic—which is considered the Super Bowl of the obedience world—attract the best working teams in the country. Amazing precision does not remove the obvious pleasure of the dog to be working with his best friend.

All of this brings the bonus of a good companion, one with enough manners to keep his nose out of the guests' cocktail glass and who waits politely for his own potato chip without too much drooling or too many mournful looks.

CANINE CITIZENSHIP

In an effort to promote responsible dog ownership and good canine members of society, the AKC approved the Canine Good Citizen Tests in 1989. We have long since passed the time

when dogs were allowed to roam at will—creating destruction, havoc and

In competition, your Bichon must perform the proper gait as well as conform to the AKC standard. Photo by Isabelle Francais.

more puppies or alternatively being fed by the butcher, the baker and the candlemaker with benign good will. Today's dog must learn to adapt to modern, crowded society.

Dogs perform the tests on leash and are graded either pass or fail. The evaluators consider the following:

1. Does this dog's behavior make him the kind of dog which they would like to own?

2. Would this dog be safe with children?

3. Would this dog be welcome as their neighbor?

4. Does this dog make his owner happy—without

At all-breed shows, the Best of Breed winner goes on to compete in the group judging.

making others unhappy?

There are ten tests. The dog must:

1. Be clean, groomed, healthy, and allow touching and brushing by the evaluator.

2. Accept a stranger's approach.

3. Walk on a loose lead under control—as though out on a walk.

4. Walk through a crowd.

5. Sit for an exam while a stranger pets him.

6. Sit and down on command.

7. Stay in position. Additionally, the entry is judged on its reaction to:

8. Another dog.

9. Distractions such as loud noises, sudden

Two beautiful babies play in the backyard.

appearance of a person or a person with an object such as a bicycle.

10. Being left alone for five minutes.

AGILITY

Agility is almost more fun than work, and it's certainly fun for those watching it. Although a few people

Winning an obedience title takes a tremendous amount of patience, hard work, and discipline on the part of Bichon and his owner.

and more American shows as well. The object is for the dog to take on each obstacle as quickly as possible and without making a mistake. These include jumps, a scaling wall, a rigid tunnel, a collapsible tunnel, a hoop, seesaw, wall, water jump and almost any other barrier a club can invent. There is also a table and a pause box, where the dog must stand on top for five seconds.

The best time and performance wins. Relay teams increase the challenge and fun. Clubs may offer courses for large dogs and for small dogs. Agility is held as a non-regular obedience class under AKC rules.

are beginning to take it seriously, most entries simply want to see if their dog can and will conquer the obstacles.

Originating in the United Kingdom in 1977, agility has begun popping up at more

THE INGREDIENTS FOR SUCCESS

Showing attracts young and old people of all shapes, sizes and ethnic origin, with their young and old dogs of all shapes, sizes and breeds. As in all situations, the human personalities vary, but the most successful dogs display confidence, enjoyment of the sport, and that elusive word "presence." Depending on the breed, a spectator might describe a dog

Though small in stature, the Bichon is more than able to compete in agility trials, with proper training.

This Bichon easily clears an 18-inch jump with no wings attached. Owner, Dolores Wolske.

as noble, regal, winsome, cute, amazing, smart or delightful. In all events, dogs displaying viciousness are disqualified.

Both owners and dogs should possess and exhibit enthusiasm for their sport, no matter what the arena. If it's not there to begin with, it sure won't be after heartbreaking defeats, treks through blizzards and dropped majors. Sometimes even hundreds of blue ribbons can make you feel blue! Therefore, whatever the sport, the main ingredient is loving dogs and doing things with them.

Flying through the tire on an agility course.

Before you purchase a Bichon Frise, you should know what a good one looks like. Photo by Isabelle Francais.

Standard for the Bichon Frise

To purchase a Bichon Frise, no less to breed a Bichon Frise, you must know precisely what a good Bichon Frise looks like. Every registering organization, such as the American Kennel Club or the Kennel Club of England, adopts an official standard for the breed, a description of what the ideal representative of the breed should look like.

Standards, like purebred dogs for the most part, are manmade and man-remade, which is to say they change over time. These "word pictures" are subject not only to change but also to interpretation. In a perfect world, every breeder is striving for the flawless dog, which is identical in every way to the next breeder's flawless dog, which is identical in every way to the next breeder's flawless dog. In reality, however, the flawless dog doesn't exist, never has and never will. Nonetheless, breeders strive to create that "perfect speciman" and smart owners strive to find that "perfect puppy."

Read the following breed standard carefully and repeatedly. Envision every part of the dog and ask an experienced breeder or exhibitor about anything you don't understand completely.

When buying a puppy, you should know what to look for and NOT to look for. Pay close attention to disqualifications and faults. When considering gait, remember that your puppy is but a "toddler"; instead observe the movement of the parents or other relatives. Structure as well as movement are passed along from parent to offspring.

GENERAL APPEARANCE—

The Bichon Frise is a small, sturdy, white powder puff of a dog whose merry temperament is

A full lineup of Bichons Frises. Photo by Robert Pearcy.

Ch. Chaminade Larkshire Lafitte, Westminster Kennel Club Best of Breed winner 1992-94. Owner, Lois Morrow. Photo by I. Francais.

evidenced by his plumed tail carried jauntily over the back and his dark-eyed inquisitive expression. This is a breed that has

The Bichon is a breed which is well balanced and has no gross or incapacitating exaggerations.

no gross or incapacitating exaggerations and therefore there is no inherent reason for lack of balance or unsound movement. Any deviation from the ideal described in the standard should be penalized to the extent of the deviation. Structural faults common to all breeds are as undesirable in the Bichon Frise as in any other breed, even though such faults may not be specifically mentioned in the standard.

Size, Proportion, Substance—

Size— Dogs and bitches $9\frac{1}{2}$ to $11\frac{1}{2}$ inches are to be given primary preference. Only where the comparative superiority of a specimen outside this range clearly justifies it should greater latitude

The most recognizable aspect of the Bichon breed is a merry temperament.

be taken. In no case, however, should this latitude ever extend over 12 inches or under 9 inches. The minimum limits do not apply to puppies.

Proportion— The body from the forward-most point of the chest to the point of rump is $\frac{1}{4}$ longer than the height at the withers. The body from the withers to lowest point of chest represents $\frac{1}{2}$ the distance from withers to ground.

Substance— Compact and of medium bone throughout, neither coarse nor fine.

Head—

1994 Westminster Winner Ch. Chaminade Larkshire Lafitte shows great proportion and balance. Owner, Lois K. Morrow.

The Bichon expression is soft, dark eyed, inquisitive, and alert. Photo by Robert Smith.

Expression— Soft, dark-eyed, inquisitive, alert. **Eyes** are round, black or dark brown and are set in the skull to look directly forward. An overly large or bulging eye is a fault as is an almond shaped, obliquely set eye. Halos, the black or very dark brown skin surrounding the eyes, are necessary as they accentuate the eye and enhance expression. The eye rims themselves must be black. Broken pigment, or total absence of pigment on the eye rims produce a bland

Ch. Chaminade Larkshire Lafitte.

legs. The lowest point of the chest extends at least to the elbow. The rib cage is moderately sprung and extends back to a short and muscular loin. The forechest is well pronounced and protrudes slightly forward of the point of shoulder. The underline has a moderate tuck-up. **Tail** is well plumed, set on level with the topline and curved gracefully over the back so that the hair of the tail rests on the back. When the tail is extended toward the head it reaches at least halfway to the withers. A low tail set, a tail carried perependicularly to the back, or a tail which

distance from forechest to buttocks. The **topline** is level except for a slight, muscular arch over the loin. **Body—** The chest is well developed and wide enough to allow free and unrestricted movement of the front

droops behind is to be severely penalized. A corkscrew tail is a very serious fault.

Forequarters— Shoulders— The shoulder blade, upper arm and forearm are approximately equal in length. The shoulders are laid back to somewhat near a forty-five degree angle. The upper arm extends well back so the elbow is placed directly below the withers when viewed from the side. **Legs** are of medium bone; straight, with no bow or curve in the forearm or wrist. The

The Bichon's plumed tail should be carried jauntily over the back. Photo by Robert Smith.

elbows are held close to the body. The **pasterns** slope slightly from the vertical. The dewclaws may be removed. The **feet** are tight and round, resembling those of a

A picture-perfect Bichon Frise. Owner, Lois Morrow. Photo by Isabelle Francais.

cat and point directly forward, turning neither in nor out. **Pads** are black. **Nails** are kept short.

Hindquarters— The hindquarters are of medium bone, well angulated with muscular thighs and spaced moderately wide. The upper and lower thigh are nearly equal in length meeting at a well bent stifle joint. The leg from hock joint to foot pad is perpendicular to the ground. Dewclaws may be removed. Paws are tight and round with black pads.

Coat— The texture of the coat is of utmost importance. The undercoat is soft and dense, the outercoat of a coarser and curlier

This Bichon displays the cat-like feet and straight legs that the standard calls for. Owner, Mimi Winkler. Photo by I. Francais.

texture, The combination of the two gives a soft but substantial feel to the touch which is similar to plush or velvet and when patted springs back. When bathed and brushed, it stands off the body, creating an overall powder puff appearance. A wiry coat is not desirable. A limp, silky coat, a coat that lies down, or a lack of undercoat are very serious faults. ***Trimming—*** The coat

The Bichon coat should be soft to the touch and create an overall powder puff appearance.

is trimmed to reveal the natural outline of the body. It is rounded off from any direction and never cut so short as to create an overly trimmed or squared off appearance. The furnishings of the head, beard, mustache, ears and tail are left longer. The longer head hair is trimmed to create an overall rounded impression. The topline is trimmed to appear level. The coat is long enough to maintain the powder puff look which is characteristic of the breed.

Color— Color is white, may have

The coat should be trimmed to reveal the natural outline of the body.

shadings of buff, cream, or apricot around the ears or on the body. Any color in excess of 10% of the entire coat of a mature specimen is a fault and should be penalized, but color of the accepted shadings should not be faulted in puppies.

Gait— Movement at a trot is free, precise, and effortless. In profile the forelegs and hind legs extend equally with an easy reach and drive

The color of the Bichon coat is white, and may have slight shadings of buff, cream or apricot.

Head study of 1995 Westminster Winner Ch. Chaminade Chamour Chances Are.

This Bichon seems to fulfill the standard's call for a gentle mannered and sensitive temperament. Photo by Paulette Braun.

that maintain a steady topline. When moving, the head and neck remain somewhat erect and as speed increases there is a very slight convergence of legs toward the center line. Moving away, the hindquarters travel with moderate width between them and the foot pads can be seen. Coming and going, his movement is precise and true.

Temperament— Gentle mannered, sensitive, playful and

A nice shot of 1994 of Westminster Winner Ch.
Chaminade Larkshire Lafitte.

affectionate. A cheerful attitude is the hallmark of the breed and one should settle for nothing less.

Approved October 11, 1988

Advancements in veterinary medicine have made it possible for your Bichon to live a long healthy life.

Prevention and Cure=A Healthy Life

Every owner hopes that his dog will live a long healthy life. Nowadays, this desire is enhanced through careful selection of puppies and breeding animals, modern technology and veterinary care and the family's care and concern—all of which aid in prevention and cure.

Dogs today are so much more fortunate than their ancestors. Regulations which were originally passed to protect property, livestock and humans actually ensure a dog's safety as well. Licenses and the accompanying taxes provide shelters for lost or abandoned animals, and a tag may prove to be a lifeline to home. Because leashes and confinement are now required by law, fewer families allow Rover to rove, and have his life ended by a bullet or highway traffic.

Many diseases commonly fatal in the early to mid-1900s are now prevented through inoculation. An old-time exhibitor understood that if he took his dog to enough shows, the animal would contract distemper sooner or later. It was common to lose entire litters to the dread disease, which plagued canines for hundreds of years. Now, thanks to nearly universal vaccination, most breeders have never even seen a case.

As recently as 1978, parvovirus swept the canine world, decimating kennels. As with all diseases, it was the very young and the very elderly dogs that succumbed in great numbers. Thanks to modern research laboratories and the pharmaceutical companies, this time within two years a preventative vaccine was available.

GENERAL MEDICAL CARE

Before a puppy is sold, he should have received at least one full set of inoculations, protecting him from distemper, hepatitis (adenovirus), leptospirosis, parainfluenza and parvo. Many breeders vaccinate against corona virus and bordatella as well. Among the puppy's stack of official papers that are turned over to the expectant parents should be a list noting the ages when additional shots will be needed.

Although the schedule varies from breeder to breeder, or one veterinarian to another, the following is an example: six weeks—combination DA2PP & Cv; nine weeks—parvo; twelve weeks—combination; sixteen weeks—parvo and rabies.

Before the puppy goes to his new home, he should be examined by a veterinarian and pronounced healthy and free of major congenital defects. Most bite, eyelid, testiculate, cardial and esophagael problems can be

Puppies should be fully examined by a veterinarian and pronounced healthy before they go to their new home.

detected before eight weeks, as can luxated patellas and open fontanels. From that point on, it's up to the new owners to continue examinations and veterinary care to keep him healthy. Routine health care, of course, includes yearly vaccinations and heartworm checks, followed by administration of the preventative.

DENTAL CARE

Dogs can't be fitted with dentures, so it's up to us to assure that their teeth last them as long as possible. Dry foods or a mixture of canned and dry help the teeth and gums remain healthy.

Feeding only moist or canned dog food can allow food to stick around the gumline, causing gums to become inflamed or teeth to decay. Even with a diet of dry food, tartar (plaque) can accumulate.

Cleaning our dog's teeth with a veterinary dentifrice, or a mixture of baking soda and water, is suggested and should be done at least once a week. The act of rubbing with a toothbrush and/or cleaning plaque with a dental tool is more important than the product used.

In this area, as well as others, never substitute your own products for those specifically made for

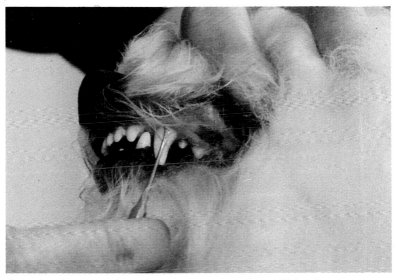

Dental maintenance is an important aspect of your Bichon's proper health care and should not be ignored.

animals without asking a veterinarian. Human toothpaste or shampoos, for example, can actually be detrimental to his care.

PARASITES

Taking stool samples to the vet should be part of the annual examination or when observing symptoms such as diarrhea, bloody stools or worm segments. Dogs, especially puppies, may vomit and lose weight when infested with parasites. Hookworms, roundworms, tapeworms, whipworms, coccidia and giardia are common. They can be eradicated with the proper medication but could be dangerous if left untreated. An over-the-counter drug may not be the right one for the particular parasite which your dog is harboring.

FLEAS

Bugs bug us and our pets. Fleas cause

Be sure your Bichon puppy receives all necessary inoculations. Remember, an ounce of prevention is worth a pound of cure.

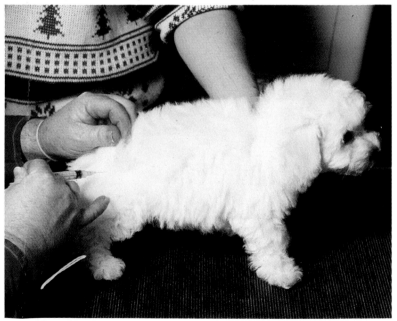

itching and carry tapeworm eggs. The resultant scratching can irritate the skin so that rashes and hot spots develop. Dogs lose hair, scratch and chew at themselves and are miserable. In attempting to exterminate the pests, owners tear their hair, scratch their heads, chew their nails and are also miserable. Better to prevent than to cure, but for everyone's sanity, once the invasion has occurred, the sooner the evacuation, the better.

Talk to your veterinarian about the proper products to use, then arrange a regular reconnaissance to prevent a losing battle with fleas. During the warm months of the year, many people spray or powder animals (including other pets who may pass fleas to your dogs) once a week and premises (house and lawn) once a month. In between, owners keep up flea surveillance. At the slightest scratch, they look for telltale evidence—skittering teeny bugs or flea dirt, which looks like a sprinkling of pepper. It's usually easiest to see the freeloaders on the less hairy groin, belly or just above the root of the tail.

Among the products used to combat flea pests are dips, collars, powders, sprays, tags and internals—drops or pills. Instructions should be followed implicitly not only for best results, but because some of these products contain ingredients which may cause problems themselves if used carelessly.

If the critters are found, shampoo or dip all dogs (cats, too, with a product labeled safe for them), and spray living and sleeping quarters. It doesn't do any good to treat the animal without debugging the environment or vice-versa. One flea who escapes will happily reinfest all over again. If the infestation is heavy, it may be necessary to fog your house and to repeat the procedure a few weeks later. All animals must be removed from the premises for the period of time specified on the fogger can.

In addition to the regular regime, many owners spray before walking dogs in areas where they are likely to pick them up, e.g., woods, pastures, training and show grounds. Most flea pesticides also kill ticks, and daily grooming sessions should include running your fingers through the dog's coat to find engorged ticks. Natural, non-insecticidal products

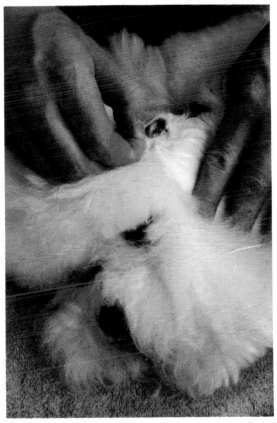

Check your Bichons ears for mites and keep the passage clean to prevent infection.

can safely be used on a daily basis in the on-going war on fleas.

LYME DISEASE

One species of tick, *Ixodes dammini*, the

tiny deer tick, is the culprit which transmits the germ that causes Lyme disease to humans and animals. Deer

Daily grooming sessions include carefully combing your Bichon's coat to remove engorged ticks.

ticks are found on mammals and birds, as well as in grasses, trees and shrubs. They are rarely visible because they are so small (as minute as the dot above an i), but the damage they can cause is magnified many times their size.

Lyme disease can damage the joints, kidneys, heart, brain and immune system in canines and humans. Symptoms can include a rash, fever, lameness, fatigue, nausea, aching body and personality change among others. Left untreated, the disease can lead to arthritis, deafness, blindness, miscarriages and birth defects, heart disease and paralysis. It may prove to be fatal.

People should cover themselves with protective clothing while outdoors to prevent bites. Repellents are helpful for both dogs and humans. Examine the body after excursions and see a doctor if symptoms appear.

SKIN DISORDERS

Dogs, just like people, can suffer from allergies. While people most often have respiratory symptoms, dogs usually exhibit their allergies through itching, scratching, chewing or licking their irritated skin.

These irritations often lead to angry, weeping "hot" spots.

Allergies are easy to detect but difficult to treat. Medications and topical substances can be useful, in addition to avoidance of the irritant, if possible.

EYES

Entropion is a condition in which the eyelid rolls inward. Eyelashes rub and irritate the cornea. In ectropion, the lower eyelid sags outward, allowing dirt to catch in the exposed sensitive area and irritate the eye. In addition, extra eyelashes grow inside the lid which rub the surface of the eye and cause tearing. Either can be treated topically or, if severe, surgically.

BONE DISEASE

Many canine bone diseases have gained nicknames—albeit not affectionate—due to the unwieldy medical terminology. For instance, canine cervical vertebral malformation/ malarticulation syndrome is referred to as "wobbler" syndrome; panosteitis is shortened to pano; and canine hip dysplasia is often simply called CHD. The first symptom is usually a limp. Diagnosis is made through a radiograph of the affected area.

Craniomandibular osteopathy (CMO) affects the growth of bone in the lower jaw, causing severe pain. Spondylosis is the technical name for spinal arthritis.

Hip dysplasia is a poor fit of the hip joint into the socket, which causes erosion. Wobbler syndrome affects the neck vertebrae, causing weakness in the hindquarters and eventually the forequarters. Osteochondrosis dissecans (OCD) affects joints, most often the shoulder, elbow or stifle. Ununited anchoneal process, commonly referred to as elbow dysplasia, is a failure of the growth line to close, thereby creating a loose piece in the joint. Kneecaps which pop out of the proper position are diagnosed as luxating patellas. Legg-Perthes, most often seen in small breeds, is a collapsing of the hip joint. They all result in the same thing: pain, lameness and, left untreated, arthritis.

The exception is pano, which is a temporary affliction causing discomfort during youth. Pano may be visible on x-rays, showing up as a cloudiness in the bone marrow in the long bones, particularly in fast-growing breeds.

Index

Page numbers in **boldface** refer to illustrations.

This is the Bichon Frise
By Joan McDonald Brearley &
Anna Nicholas
PS-700
ISBN 0-87666-247-5
UPC 0-18214-62475-2
Contains History, insights into
purchasing, General Care and
Management, plus other relevant
information.
HC, 5 ½ X 8", 320 pages, B & W,
over 170 full color photos.

Bichon Frise
By Martin Weil
KW-140
ISBN 0-7938-1155-4
UPC 0-18214-67396-5
Contains sensible, easy-to-follow
recommendations about selecting
and caring for a Bichon Frise.
224 pages, over 200 full color
photos and drawings.